This Poem Here

Rob Walton

your support!

Rob Walton

ARACHNE PRESS

First published in UK 2021 by Arachne Press Limited
100 Grierson Road, London SE23 1NX
www.arachnepress.com
© Rob Walton 2021
ISBNs:
Print 978-1-913665-30-2
ePub 978-1-913665-31-9
Mobi/Kindle 978-1-913665-32-6
The moral rights of the author have been asserted.
All content is copyright the author.
All rights reserved. This book is sold subject to the condition that it shall not by way of trade or otherwise, be lent, resold, hired out or otherwise circulated without the publisher's prior written consent in any form or binding or cover other than that in which it is published and without similar condition including this condition being imposed on the subsequent purchaser.

Except for short passages for review purposes no part of this publication may be reproduced, stored in a retrieval system or transmitted in any form, or by any means, electronic, mechanical, photocopying, recording or otherwise without prior written permission of Arachne Press Limited.

Thanks to Muireann Grealy for her proofing.

Thanks to Paul Summers for his cover design.

Printed on wood-free paper in the UK by TJ Books Limited, Padstow.

This Poem Here

For my dad, Frank Walton
5.8.33 – 24.5.20

Contents

This Poem Here	7
Hey Dude, Don't Diss Don's Disinfectant Facts	8
Frailty	9
Covey	10
Every Time	11
Visitors	12
Who You Are	13
Meaning	14
Dilute to Taste	15
Howick to Craster and Back	16
Routine	17
Dream Catcher	18
Like in the Olden Days	19
Unforgiving	20
Self-aware	21
Lockdown Pint	22
Implausible	23
June 1st	24
The Class of 2020	25
Applause	27
One Man and His Dog	28
Breadhead	29
Waiting (i)	30
And in Lockdown	31
The Great British Pub	32
Lockdown Research	33
Waiting (ii)	34

Where Have All the Quizzes Gone?	35
Toilet Tissue	36
It's a Rich Gardeners' World	37
Last Night's Quiz	38
One of the Very Worst Things	39
House Beautiful	40
Eve is Not in Dubrovnik	41
2021 Oxbridge Entrance Exam	42
What Do You Do?	43
Pinpointed	44
Dawning	45
The Last Dance	46
#UKPLCXMAS2020	47
Prime Minister's Questions	48

This Poem Here

Christ, if I went through all the regrets
I have about my dad and the things
I could and should have done
I'd write poem after poem after book
and it would be a full collection
dissected in some online journal
or some blog and recommended
to someone's 167 twitter followers.

God, if I went through all the regrets
I had about my dad when I was a full-grown adult
it would make an award-avoiding pamphlet
that one person would ask me to sign
and I'd spell their name wrong
even after I'd carefully asked them.

Jesus, if I were to write about the fact
my dad saw me in some strange pantomimes
and acting the goat on other stages
and even telling so-called jokes on the boards
of Kinsley Labour Club and how I regret
he never saw me reading poetry
never saw me reading poems
in celebration of him and my mum
well that

That would be a poem.
That would be this poem here.
That he'd never read.
That he'd never hear.

Hey Dude, Don't Diss Don's Disinfectant Facts
(24th April, 1:56 p.m. after a POTUS speech)

A dose of Dettol
will hopefully settle
all your ailments.

Consider Cillit Bang
as the cure-all thang
for Covi – for cron – for the bigly virus.

A vial of bleach
administered to each
and every one of us
will cure every everything.

What could be neater
than Sainsbury's citrus bleach
at 87p a litre?

A dram of Domestos
is the best loss
leader in all top pharmacies.

Harpic white and shine
is simply divine
and recommended by all top doctors.

Duck deep action gel
will not make your organs swell.

And finally, folks, remember –
Zoflora and Jeyes Fluid are buggers to rhyme.

Frailty

is written on the certificate
below Covid
but no frailty was found
in the Wolverhampton marathon at fifty
or the Lincs half mile at seventeen.

Little was found jogging and walking
in Beadnell at eighty
and none was found
holding my mum
and the four of us
or working
a double shift
in the light and dark
of the furnace.

Covey
(May 24th, 9:24 a.m.)

So Covey –
you don't mind if I call you Covey?
be my guest
So how you doing?

pretty bored
been trying to get in to some pubs
but they're all closed
i'd love to snuggle up to a drinker
or a diner

Can't you just go somewhere else?
i thought about schools
what i wouldn't give
for a close encounter with a caretaker
or a classroom assistant
but they don't let me in

What, there's like barriers?
well, more of a mumbled request
and a throwaway wish

So you're staying away?

biding my time, mate
biding my time

Every Time

I go into my daughter's room
which is usually to take her toast
or an iced latte
or a treat
I catch sight of the photo of my dad and her
she has stuck to the wall above her desk
and I exit
pursued by something hard to bear

Visitors

Prince George as was
visited Scunthorpe in 1933,
the year my dad was born.

I watched a film of it
on BFI Player in 2020,
the year my dad died.

Back on the day in '33 when the prince visited
the wind were that bloody strong
folk were having to hold on to their hats.

Folk were holding on to all sorts.
Everything was in danger of being blown away.

The prince visited the hospital
where my dad worked
until he was sixty-five,
and returned to when he was eighty-six.

Folk are holding on to all sorts.
Everything is in danger of being blown away.

Who You Are

that young woman
who came with me
to the funeral
is who you are

I thought you were a teenager
in love with her phone

that young woman
who held my hand
at the funeral
is who you are

I thought you were a teenager
in love with her phone

that young woman
who cried with me
at the funeral
is who you are

You are all that
and so much more.

Meaning

I was looking for meaning on the A1058
from Newcastle to the coast.
I was looking for meaning on the A19
from the Tyne Tunnel towards home.
I was looking for meaning on the A15
the old Roman road to or from Lincoln.
I thought I might have found the meaning
I was looking for
at Caenby Corner
but it was just a shut-down transport café
I used to drive past with my parents.

Dilute to Taste

Returning from a mad dogs and Englishmen midday run
spent thinking about this and that
this being the love I have for my mum
that being the sadness I feel about not being with her
I dilute some orange squash
pouring the cold water into an inch
of orange at the bottom of the bottle and that smell
for someone with a terrible sense of it
is anytime forty or fifty years ago of the squash
my mum
would have diluted
with full-strength love

Howick to Craster and Back

Before the walk
from Howick to Craster
or maybe after
Phil tells me he's waiting
to take delivery of a bracelet
that will project his phone's screen
on to his arm.
I'm not sure I believe him.

On the walk
from Howick to Craster
or maybe on the way back
Sarah tells me ponies
are more intelligent than horses.
Is this a fact?
How did they prove this?
Can ponies have web pages
projected on to their wrists
or fetlocks or whatever you call them?

On the drive back
from Longhoughton to Whitley Bay
my wrist vibrates.
I pull into a lay-by
and look down at my arm
to receive my first update
about the relative intelligences
and gullibilities
of donkeys, asses
ponies, horses, and poets.

Routine

I will get up in the morning
crying fragile damaged
and make myself two cups of tea
and I will take them back to bed
and read and surf
then I will go downstairs
fragile damaged crying
and I will make another cup of tea
chop a banana
sort out some cereal
and go back to bed
and I will continue doing *Routine* things
like this throughout the day
and I will continue feeling *damaged fragile*
will continue *crying*
and wish another *Routine* for all of us

Dream Catcher

This dream catcher on my Velux window
was found somewhere
possibly by some Whitley Bay elder
and I have no idea if dream catchers
are for good dreams or bad dreams
and what if like I have
what if it's say caught my daughter's dreams and
she wants me dead
and what if it was from a charity shop
and it's bringing other people's unwanted dreams
into my room in my house
and is it just the sleepy sleep dreams
or is it the hopes and dreams
the ones that are as tatty as the worn out
Velux window dream catcher

Like in the Olden Days

I want my daughters' friends to come for tea
I want to serve them uninteresting pasta
with a jar of Aldi tomato sauce
and some veggie parmesan
and maybe
I don't know
a coke float
or an ice cream
or pretty much anything really
I just want my daughters' friends
to come for tea

like in the olden days
you know
like in the olden days

Unforgiving

Steve bikes over
and lends me **K-Tel's**
40 Super-greats
40 Top Ten Hits
Superb 2 LP Set
as advertised on TV and Radio
with Gary Glitter and
one or two artists
who will be remembered
mostly for their music.

What Steve doesn't tell me is that he's
put record 1 at the back
of the gatefold sleeve
where record 2 should go.

I've come across some sly tricks
in my fifty six years
but this takes the fucking biscuit.

Self-aware

If there's one thing
I'm good at doing
in a crisis
it's not getting
round to doing stuff
in a crisis.

Lockdown Pint

I went on WhatsApp
and said I fancied a pint
of beer in a pub

I went past a bar when I was exercising
and it made me want to go in
and have a pint of beer

I had a Zoom meeting and mentioned
that I fancied a pint
in a nice beer garden

I told someone
in a Messenger video
that I could murder a pint

Had to make do with twelve cans of Stella
and a Christmas pudding
in bed

Implausible

The stress levels of school children have been
implausibly high.
Children have been put under implausibly high levels of stress.
Teachers have for years been given implausibly low pay rises.
The care and professionalism shown by support staff has been
implausibly high.
Other education staff's diligence in these times has been
implausibly high.
The graft of the cleaners and caretakers has been
implausibly high.
The awareness and compassion of the welfare staff has been
implausibly high.
The patience of the admin staff has been
implausibly high.
The flexibility of cooks and lunchtime staff has been
implausibly high.
For years the pay rises of teachers have been
implausibly low.

Excuses offered by the government have been implausible.

(The infamous algorithm was meant to moderate the process of awarding grades, to prevent teachers awarding marks to pupils that the exams watchdog described as 'implausibly high'.)

The Class of 2020

I saw those Instagram photos
of your improvised last day
and I saw the love between
and the sadness between
and the togetherness between
and I saw the class
of young people being between
this thing and another thing

I saw the dates of Lenin's reign
and German verbs
on your bedroom wall
over the ghosts of photos
of festivals and parties

I saw crossed-out dates
and wallchart entries
colour coding and *cancelled*
and countless question marks

I saw the rug pulled
and the plug pulled
and someone you didn't choose
pulling people down

I saw TikTok likes
and FaceTime faces
on a laptop screen in a bedroom
over doorstep presents
and undelivered hugs

I saw real friends
with pixelated laughs and smiles
and very clean hands
and I saw the love between
and the sadness between
and the togetherness between
and I saw the Class of 2020

June 1st

What did you do on your first day back, darling?

Lick Yusuf.

Oh, right, and what did Yusuf do?

Nothing. Him on top of Shira.

Mmm. And did Ms Key do anything about this?

Couldn't. Twins stuck on her legs.

The Alton twins?

*No, them in helper's hair,
play with him mask.*

And how do you feel about going back tomorrow?

Stay home. Watch stupid men on telly.

Applause

one day, one winter
I clapped my daughter
as she ran past me
in a school cross country race

I ran across the field
to clap at another point
where they crossed a path
going from the public field
to a lap of the high school field

then I tried to run and film her
but I fell short

a couple of years later
I am running on the path
between the public field and the high school
as students return after six months

I want to clap them
I want to applaud them
as they stand with friends
all nervous excitement
well not all nervous excitement
there's probably already some boredom
and a couple of vendettas
but you know whatever
I want to clap
I want to clap

One Man and His Dog

One man went to see
went to see a poet
One man and his dog
went to see a poet.

Two men went to see
went to see a poet
Two men, one man and his dog
went to see a poet.

Three men went to see
went to see a poet –
Sorry. I got a bit
carried away there.

Breadhead

Tom in Aldi says the Ancient Grains
Farmhouse loaf is only 89p.

I tell him I'm willing to pay
up to ninety-five pence

if he's got something a bit more modern
and with an urban setting.

Waiting (i)

I have not been waiting
in the waiting room
of the doctor/dentist/car repair place

I have not been waiting
and because I have not been waiting
I have saved at least an hour

An hour which I spent yearning
to wait in the waiting room
of the doctor/dentist/car repair place

And in Lockdown

and in lockdown
it seems perfectly reasonable
to get tearful
over the Jersey Royals
untouched and forgotten about
in the cupboard under the sink

and now the girls
have gone back to their mum's
you'll have the Jersey Royals
on your own
on their own
or with a bit of butter
but snide Lurpak
won't help them pass
the lump in your throat

The Great British Pub

I had a lovely pub lunch today –
me and a Ploughman
and Betty Turpin,
who'd burnt the hotpots –
in The Olde Bloke's Head

I had a single malt
in one of them big fancy new glasses
and a bit joke with the barman
in the White Lying

I had a pint of Marston's Pedigree
some of which missed my mouth
and ruefully reminisced
in the Cock and Bull

Two pints of IPA
and a shiny crisp packet
pulled apart on the table
like a fancy sharing platter
in the Royal Joak

Got accused of not being able
to hold my beer
and being a bit of a fantasist
in The Ravellers Rest

Lockdown Research

tells me that
INCREDIBLY!
Worcestershire is a real place

I'd thought it was like one of those farms
from where budget supermarkets
claim to get their milk
or Cornish pasties or granola

But it exists
more or less between
the reassuringly fictional
'Northumberland' and 'East Riding of Yorkshire'

Footnote: Cornish is an adjective
derived from Cornwall
a county created by hungry Virginia Woolf
for her essay
A Pasty of One's Own

Waiting (ii)

Because I have not been waiting in waiting rooms
I have missed the opportunity to read
someone else's discarded magazines

I have not found out about my pectoral inadequacies
in an abandoned copy of Men's Health

I have not found out about the One Show
presenter's newly discovered love of beetroot

I still don't know about the year-on-year sales growth
of vegan ready meals in the different countries
of the United Kingdom

And I do not read about what has happened
to the waiting room magazines
I can no longer steal

Where Have All the Quizzes Gone?

Where will all the quiz questions go
when the virus is gone?

Who will be asked whether the UK
has a larger population than France?
(Answer: Sometimes).

Who will be responding to whether
Harrison Ford's previous job was
a) carpenter
b) Carpenter
or
c) Anita Dobson?

Who will be 100% sure about
percentages?

Who won't have a clue about
a one-time host of Give us a Clue?

Which one of us will have a stab in the dark
about the origin of the expression *stab in the dark*?

What will we do with all the questions?

Where will we find some answers?

Toilet Tissue

I have considered, he said,
popping up to Aldi, he said.

I may purchase, he said,
my first roll of toilet tissue
since lockdown, he said.

I have an overwhelming feeling
of enterprise
and achievement, he said,

placing a small sticker on his lapel
and writing his own name
on a certificate.

It's a Rich Gardeners' World

We're having a crowd-funder
up our street
trying to raise funds
so that one of us
can buy one of the big terracotta pots
Monty Don's always casually walking past
on Gardeners' World
on a Friday night.

We've got 120 contributors
so nearly halfway there.

Last Night's Quiz

Without checking, can you remember
if it was on Messenger, Skype, WhatsApp
or filmed live by the ghost
of Trevor McDonald's dad
and Steph McGovern in your living room?

Did you prefer the third glass
of Shiraz or the fourth?
And were you remotely bothered
that the tilting glass and your tilting head
kept coming into shot?

Did you come in the top three
or were you soundly beaten
by two imaginary cousins
and that sexy plumber
from a suburb of Antwerp
that none of you knew or invited?

Was that a little bit of sick on your collar?

What do you think caused the noise
that stopped you from hearing
the Food and Drink round
when you were eating Lime
and Coriander Chutney Poppadom Sensations
dipped in crushed Doritos?

Would you come again?

One of the Very Worst Things

One of the very worst things
to happen to me in lockdown
was the Zoom meeting where
I knocked the video function off
and changed my shirt
then put the video back on.

I did this seven times
and no-one noticed.

House Beautiful

There are some weirdos out there
participating in online poetry readings
and these so-called participants
are actually listening to the poets
instead of scrolling through
and checking the expressions
and clothing of the other participants
and having a good nosey through their
so-called *living* quarters.

Eve is Not in Dubrovnik

Eve is not in Dubrovnik
Emily is not in Gdansk
My daughter is not in Llubljana
Sarah is not in Split

But they are with each other
in gardens
in gin
in raspberry mojitos
in half-hearted limbo dancing

They are with each other
in the hope next year
travel might broaden the mind
and narrow the savings

So Sarah will be in Split
My daughter will be in Llubljana
Emily will be in Gdansk and
Eve will be in Dubrobnik

2021 Oxbridge Entrance Exam

Ethics Paper
In the 2020 A Level Clusterfuck who did Gavin Williamson hate most?
(a) teenagers
(b) parents
(c) teachers
(d) all of the above
For a bonus point, complete the following.
That unspeakable Johnson fucked off on another holiday because

_____

What Do You Do?

What do you do if your career path
is dug up for essential maintenance?
What do you do if the road ahead
is closed?
What do you do if you see a sign that says
delays possible (up to two years)?
What do you do if you see the contact number
for life's highways department and you can't get
through?
What do you do if you can't get through?
What do you do if you paid attention
in all the driving lessons
and know the Highway Code backwards
and you followed all the rules
and there's a sign that says road narrows
and then yet another sign that says road narrows
and then a sign that says the lane is closed?
What do you do if
there's a load of members of the government in hi-vis
on the hard shoulder
giving you the finger?
What do you do?
Really, what the fuck do you do?

Pinpointed

at 3:37 p.m.
on an August
not august
Thursday
the saddest
I have ever been.

Though the time is recorded
without my watch
which has stopped
would you Adam & Eve it
proper stopped
and the time is recorded
without my phone
which – never the bearer
of good news –
has been left
like me

somewhere or other

Dawning

One November Sunday at 12:40 p.m.
I realise there is no guarantee
that Hilary Hahn will leave her violin,
her two children, her husband
and her Cambridge, Massachusetts home
to come and help me sort
out the shelves and the punctured bike tyre
in the shed in Whitley Bay.

There is, it dawns on me, a chance
she will not know how thickly to butter the bread
for a crisp sandwich.

Playing *The Lark Ascending* so exquisitely
might not necessarily equip her
for a half-time Guinness at Hillheads.

It's obviously a blow, but better I know now
before I take the key to the padlock
and put enough water in the kettle for two mugs.

The Last Dance

Dominic's dancing in his Death Star t-shirt
Smooching with mammon, digging up real dirt

His henchmen have got the DJ pissed
Altered the algorithms on his bangin' playlist

He sniggers with Gavin when they go to the bogs
Talks about the après-prom round at Rees-Mogg's

Chats about roubles and hilarious Debs
And pissing on the prospects of the oiks and the plebs

Here's Grant guffawing, and shuffling 'cross the floor
Ignoring the commotion outside the twice-locked door

*If you've got a complaint you know where you can stick it
You can't come in here with a third class ticket.*

#UKPLCXMAS

Three Christmas puddings are allowed to meet
but only in a manger.
Welsh gin can be mixed with tonic
and drunk by a Scottish stranger.

You can have mistletoe with a substantial meal
but you must bring your own crackers.
Holly wreaths are allowed on composite doors.
Fake snow can be sprayed on knackers.

Carols can be sung behind your masks
provided you're pissed and tuneless.
Gabriel can appear from up above
as long as the night is moonless.

The Northern Irish can put up trees –
a fir or a spruce for instance.
Tinsel is allowed in any colour.
Baubles should keep social distance.

Santa will be helped by two English deer
pulling a sleigh and a geet big sack.
The presents you get will be quite shit
but at least they'll be traced and tracked.

Prime Minister's Questions

Are there any other countries you'd like to break?
If you grow it out a bit, would you like me to cut it into a bob?
Do you miss the *good old days* of racist newspaper columns?
Is the dandruff cultivated to evoke sympathy?
Will you answer the question about the inflatable Cummings?
Do you understand the difference between a million
and a billion?
Who's your favourite bully?
How about a nice lie-down?
Who's spaffing now?
Could you tell the House which of his houses your dad is in
at the moment?
Is it the Ready Brek that makes you glow inside?
Have you got Brexit done?
Do you miss the *good old days* of the zip wire and the flags?

Are there any other countries you'd like to break?